PRAISE FOR DAVID WOO'S *Divine Fire*:

Divine Fire is even better than *The Eclipses*, praising which I pretty much used up my store of superlatives. It's funnier, sexier, wiser, more grief-stricken, more profoundly literary, more personal without ever once stooping to mere revelation. It makes me think of that remark of Mallarmé's about all earthly existence belonging in a book—or, as tweaked by Merrill in *The Book of Ephraim*, "the world was made to end (*pour aboutir*) / in a slim volume." In fact, a very apt comparison can be made with *Ephraim*, despite their obvious differences: it feels more and more, with each rereading, like an entire life, "a sea to swim in," one I sense I will never quite get to the bottom of, or want to.

—DANIEL HALL, author of *Under Sleep*

David Woo's quietly magisterial, wide-rangingly allusive second book of poems *Divine Fire* stations us like the man Kafka imagined in front of a mirror containing all of the world's wisdom, but unlike that man who "desired . . . to ensure . . . the silvering" properties of the mirror would last—a kind of fool's errand—Woo shows us a way through the chimera of the world's wisdom to a "real life . . . mirror . . . nailed to the ceiling" of "some red-velvet motel," beneath which we move achingly aware of "all those limbs" before us, with us, that have knotted and unknotted in the "art of becoming another." What we see in the "real life" mirror is not world wisdom but a divine fire that both makes and destroys us so that "what remains is something wee, / wee and oh-so-sempiternal, the self / unselfing another, world without end."

—MICHAEL COLLIER, author of *My Bishop and Other Poems*

PRAISE FOR DAVID WOO'S POETRY:

David Woo's poems have an empty-room silence in them in which you can hear things he only half-way wants you to, and a brimming gorgeousness that can tip without warning into something scoured and simple.

—KAY RYAN

Among the most achieved first books I've ever seen, absolutely standing in its own ripened voice and heart, a perfect, rare marriage of language perception and feeling

—JANE

DIVINE
FIRE

GEORGIA
REVIEW
BOOKS

EDITED BY
GERALD MAA

DIVINE FIRE

POEMS

DAVID WOO

THE UNIVERSITY OF
GEORGIA PRESS
ATHENS

Published by the University of Georgia Press
Athens, Georgia 30602
www.ugapress.org
© 2021 by David Woo
All rights reserved
Designed by Kaelin Chappell Broaddus
Set in 10.2/17 Janson Text LT Std 55 Roman
by Kaelin Chappell Broaddus
Printed and bound by Sheridan Books, Inc.
The paper in this book meets the guidelines for
permanence and durability of the Committee on
Production Guidelines for Book Longevity of the
Council on Library Resources.

Most University of Georgia Press titles are
available from popular e-book vendors.

Printed in the United States of America
25 24 23 22 21 P 5 4 3 2 1

Library of Congress Control Number: 2020947854
ISBN: 9780820358840 (pbk.: alk. paper)
ISBN: 9780820358857 (ebook)

FOR THOSE WHO
RETURNED ME TO LIFE
IN THEIR LIVING FIRE:
Daniel R., Eric, Didi,
David, and Sweet William

Contents

DIVINE
FIRE

AMBIENT LIFE

You have invited some friends over for dinner,
and each of them has brought along one or two friends,
who each brought one or two more, until the room
is crowded and senseless,

and the roast is being hacked and impaled
on toothpicks as makeshift hors d'œuvres,
and wine glasses blithely tossed into the fireplace,

and a drunken stranger is cavorting on a giant mobile
outside your bedroom window. By now you've given up

trying to control anyone. You lie in bed, listening
to the sounds of a party that is nonsensical to you
and brings you no pleasure. A police siren

comes closer and closer, then dopplers into silence.
The hydraulics of a bus sighs rudely. A washing machine
merges into a pack of feral dogs. I meant to ask you

a question at the party, but I see now that you're tucked in,
except for the pajamas with bunny feet that peek out
from under the covers. How small you are, how helpless.

I kiss you goodnight, once on each eye, and wipe away
the last tears from your lifelong tantrum.
Then I close the door slowly, slowly,

to avoid making any noise.

ON BEING ASKED
WHAT'S NEW

Nothing's new anymore. The vellum of a face
on which is written, "Forty years, half a century."
I know that the volcano Laki caused a famine
in 1783, but I still haven't seen Reykjavík.
I'm always in the same Zen garden trying to turn
the raked sand into an ocean. Why do I wonder
if I'll ever be as elegant as the cheap Andean
handkerchief in my pocket? So many roses,
so little love. I stopped traveling, except in books.
Behind my father's house is the bamboo grove
where he played. "You should observe
the faces of children," Wittgenstein advised.
I think of you most on Saturday evenings,
after it's rained, and the air in the garden is new.

ON TRYING TO
FORGET SOMEONE

Or the divination stick stuffed in a dusty backpack
by a Dogon priest as memento of those perished years;

or the soft gnocco of an earlobe, the ardent way
it lingers under a sidewalk amplifier wafting *Erbarme dich*;

or the sweet echolalia of a tag question, as if to say,
"Darling, I'm listening, listening, aren't I?"

or the last glimpse of an arm through a closing door,
plangent as a tanka tucked in a Heian lover's sleeve:

if I distilled all qualities to one, in final valediction,
in the last Eros of shriving, if I confessed one by one

that I willed to forget one by one, as a wilted rose
discards the evidence of its beauty one by one,

what would there be left to love but myself alone?
And how to be alone if not in leaving myself to love?

ON REFUSING TO
BE ON THE MAKE

If I had turned around at the right time and seen
what was behind me, I would know
what my actions meant: that everything served
the same cause, and was known to serve the same cause,

as if I were transparent and could see motives
flowing through me, like a picture frame held
over a trout-filled stream. Now I must go on walking

and walking along these blind paths where dreams
no longer exist because the self itself has gone clear.
On the bridge in autumn, leaves are falling from trees
I can no longer see. Lovers are holding hands

that carry invisible photo albums of the families
they will never have.

But I am walking on, for once, without questioning
what lies behind. As for the future, how can I help
but judge you by how gracefully you brush aside
the falling leaves?

Or how selflessly you turn to me and remove one
clinging to the small of my back.

SEQUEL

They are gazing at the movies from the lawn,
their eyes in unison, following the man
who kisses the woman, who kisses him back

then slaps him across the face with such force
the breeze rustles the screen, which turns out to be

the curtain of your bedroom, where you look out
at the strange faces in the yard, the woman
weeping over what you have done, the angry man

rustling through the leaves as he storms away,
and the child among them who doesn't understand

and doesn't care, but who stares at your features
and those of your lover reclining behind you,
asleep, or dead, or dying, as if to memorize them

for the day he's old enough to enact the story himself,
repeating your mistakes, making a few of his own,
until the lights come up and the audience trickles away.

FOR LOVE

(AFTER *TWELFTH NIGHT*)

The air that ranges over the present without judgment,
the sun that picks the gillyflower and oxlip gold,
the casement ensphered in the lit orb of a pearl—
I cannot reach for love, I cannot touch for love.
The glass would cut my hand, and sun would burn
my petals, and air would judge my folly with a gust.
Even at the Elephant, searching for Antonio,
I wandered the cobblestone of the inn-yard hearing
no words issue from the actors' mouths, no sizzle
from the torches, no *holla!* from the vintner:
Antonio passed through me, searching for me;
I was ghosted for love. Outside, the black taxi
took me along the river, and I, fingering all along
the jewel in my pocket, saw tableaux of decay, fall
of buildings, bombs, pendulum of wrecking balls,
then the rise of cranes, of steel-girder acrobats,
beyond the gaze of a mere taxi window. How clear
you'd become, backlit with stars, in a blue high-rise
fixed darkly on the fulcrum of our nakedness.
If I lower the curtain here, we will never be clothed.

THE EMPATH

I found myself in another body, gazing at a greenish sky,
tinted lenses shifting the spectrum a shade
to the left. Now I was looking angrily at myself—

at the birthmark on my arm and the strain in my eyes
as I felt your words reverberating from within
your throat. I could not stop you from saying the things

you said, but I could feel your reasons for saying them,
why you chose to be cruel, why you ended each sentence
with that mocking, basilisk grin—ah, the kindness

of refusing to prolong the inevitable. The car that drove by
was the same, only angled to my side, and the stranger
who rolled down the window to ask me for directions

was the same, only I could feel your displaced anger
as she whispered with welcome kindness, "I'm so sorry
for interrupting," and turned forever and drove away.

ON THE SKIN OF
THE CUTTLEFISH

If my words shivered over my skin, shimmered back
as moiré, as pointillé, in crinkled foil layers
of blue-sequined chitin, or enbulbed themselves

like lights along the length of my torso, scurfed
and burning in ocellate riffles of embodied syntax,
like a flowing installation by Jenny Holzer,

if irony was forbidden, and subtext, if meaning
was meaning alone, in the eloquence of the flesh
(its electric siren song, its poignant interference pattern

of appetite, of rage, of tenderness), if my colors
betrayed my feeling before I knew what I had felt,
each color telling the history of my affections,

the noblesse oblige of ocher, the learned helplessness
of crimson, how my skin's muscled chromatophores
contracted round the hues and tints of your body,

how my green-blue blood murmured our love
in infinite permutation, high and low, in tidal swell
and mangrove swamp, among the brain coral

and on the feather-down coral bed, I would wish
for surface, for my fathoms to plumb a shallow strand,
I would covet no inner life, no enigma of otherness,

no touchstone of alienation, only the pulse arrow
of desire expelled from flesh, telling us all we knew
of the other, raw, fleeting, and forever skin-deep.

DARKER

There was a time that was easeful to the mind.
You didn't have to think, you just did or were.
You got on a train and there you were.
You went to work and there you were.
The architecture of the building was yours,
and the boss may have been exigent but he was yours.
Certainly the neighbors were yours, and the newspapers
were filled with you. If you liked art and books
they were always yours. If you liked sports,
the players and the coaches and the rules
were nothing but you at your golden best.
If you were thoughtless, you could sit in an easy chair,
knowing the TV would smile its gorgon smile
and disgorge images of you and you and you.
And your wife—who else could she be but yours,
in every turn of her apron, in every turn of her duster
on the banister, in every pliant turn in bed?
Thought, thought is the enemy, or the thought
that represses a thought. To be self-conscious,
to go through life assessing each habit, phrase,
way of looking, to know that the neutral expression
on your face will always be misconstrued
as scornful or insufficiently respectful,

to avoid being the Other in the room,

to avoid saying the one thing that would surround you

in a fetid cloud of loathing, to have to think not to think!

Look at your hand—isn't it changing from all

the repression? Look at your face—

that isn't a five o'clock shadow

but something deeper and more permanent,

something—dare I say it?—darker, darker,

something you can never scrub off.

ON REFUSING TO CLICK ON
IMAGES OF NATURAL DISASTERS

They arrived in a land where the stone-faced imperatives
of order and authority no longer existed. Stones
replaced them. Stone once removed—stone made from stone,
breccia, sandstone—replaced neighbors and friends,

and spoke the inhuman language of stones, full of deep
implausible sounds, like continuous, voiced, epiglottal plosives.

In your little house, you are free and thoughtless as a stone,
your doors unlatched, your windows open.
Today you meant to enjoy the air, freshly scrubbed
by days of rain, but find yourself expelling

affected, oddly foreshortened breaths,
as if repeating a language lesson from a country
floating in the ether.

Above you someone important is circling in a helicopter,
and he waves to you. You wave back jauntily,
then look down and notice that you are clinging
to a roof, a tree, a mound of rubble.

But you can see his face in close-up on a million screens.
He is wiping away an invisible tear,
and his helicopter never rescues you.

THE LEAF BLOWER AMONG
THE SWIMMING POOL LIGHTS

From inside your headphones, behind the chirring decibels,
the white rumble of stars, syncopation of falling stars,
the artifice of a blue cosmos in illuminated water—

you are late for home, late for the mangoes and the rice.
Each movement you make parts another family's serenity,
parts it and restores it to the clear, aside a pyramid of leaves.

Chaise longue, splayed oak, sprinkler's translucent gravity.
Is it for them you bind exigencies with a bow and release
to thoughtless pastoral the flat, green essence of a lawn?

If inside you is a blue pool full of stars, it is never yours.
You own only the specter of coins in someone else's yard:
a garden's footlights, a blue moon, a watery constellation.

Who is she but your young wife holding aloft a scallop shell
of marble spilling water in the dusk? You would hold her,
and in the vigil of your arms you would vanquish the dust

of the world by carting it closer to where she awaits you,
owning it, inhabiting it, with her, aside her, at the dusty pale
of the city, dove shot sleeking and spinning a bright tin can.

THE LEAF BLOWER
IN THE DUST STORM

Pero la vida es tuya:
surge y ama.
LUIS CERNUDA

Inside the room of the body you bide the air's self-doubt
with a red-bandanna mask under goggle and headphone,
your senses bated, the whirlwind machine at your side.
Through a leather glove you finger the switch to dream
the clownish redundancy of whirling leaf on whirling leaf.
But life is yours: arise and love.

Leaf-shaped, palmately lobed, the dust fisks your bare edges,
dream-burrowing into the starlit fissures of the mind
sidereal reminders of man's origins as light from clash of dust.
Phonemes ("the bat from Dis in this vat") burble up from
constant
self-doubt, telescoped daily in querulous gazes and alien faces.
Yet life is yours: arise and love.

Face of one who loves you, face of *alma*, of epithalamium's
constancy, face of one comprising clean gesture and radiant
dust bathed one day in your liquid hands as Eros's transitory
mind retains image on image, the wash basin, the blue-green
edges of tile in her parents' kitchen, where you fell for her,
since life was yours: you rose and loved.

15

And Love will wait for the man stilled in the center of a
	storm.
Blue wisps of sky whorl back to dust, like green summer grass
transitory under your boots. So much of a day is imagined
radiance, the house you'll buy, guitar for strumming
epithalamia to your love, loves of friends, the fallen world,
	after life is yours, and you rise and love.

World dislocated, poor lost Adam among the dirt and leaves
strumming their plaint about endless loss and ravaged hopes,
imagine something more than the wind's vitriol and bitter
	asides:
grass in your own yard, "Milonga del Ángel" on your
	headphones,
storms gone, Eve at home, the dust no longer abrading your
	dream
	that life is yours to arise and love.

ON FAILING TO WRITE
A POEM AGAINST WAR

Not a battlefield but a metaphor for battles
in the plain room adorned with cut-out silhouettes
of a family lost in an argument without origin,

not a massacre but wounds of tenderness
to be bandaged, made aseptic, someday
forgotten, even the scar ignored when exposed,

not a bullet, not a fire burst, not a fléchette
gyring out of the trench into the open mouth
of some whirling, voracious, flying machine,

I saw no vision, ink-stained with searching one,
my hands glazed on the friction of my ablutions,
clear laminate of my palms, cleansed lifeline,

eyes lost in a thousand liquid prisms, the way
water takes you into its course to pacify you now,
as it invades the air, with its slow vanishing.

AFTER READING
THE *ZIBALDONE*

Walking the reservoir path alone, the others
inside watching the game, even the songbirds
gone to where songbirds go, I ask myself

how often I've circled the water, noting the flickers
that turn on a breeze, multifarious and yet
the same, and told myself, "This is true peace,"

which like any passing truth is also untrue
for others or myself another time, an illusion
I nurtured "to be better filled with solitude."

And though it gives way to low and muted light,
to a sun so heavy with trees I see no flickers
but one opaquely vanishing lake, still I

feel peace when the game ends, and joggers return,
striding to the bass thumps in their earphones,
and I hear him whisper of Virgil's nightingale,

which grieved the loss of its young with no desire
for revenge, singing purely as Orpheus did
after his loved one flickered away in the dark.

THE WORDS

In the novel a story unspools in lines,
tangled vines crumple from the chill,
and words clear the view to the mountains
with an absence of words: no houses, no roads.

There a newly released wolf is sniffing
the ground for first prey, among snow drifts
punctuated with burnt pinecones.
The word *restraint* disrobes above a hot spring.

Far from the secret airstrip where white dust
burns the nostrils with the folly of dollars,
down to the alcove under a meadow
where the dispossessed hide with field mice,

the words lace up their aglets along lines
knotted and knotted to no end except
The End, like the shoes of a dead man
tied in the casket by a delicate stranger.

I close the book and reach for a letter unopened
for days, not forgotten, not untouched,
as if it were something growing within me,
something I can palpate with rising terror.

The basket of cloudberries and dill still sits
on my desk, made of someone else's words.
The letter opener gleams in my hand.
If I read the words, my life will happen.

THE DEATH OF
THE FAMILY POEM

If I built a stone wall, if I rebuilt a premodern wall
rebuilt for millennia, if my fingertips bled from asperities
exposed by capillary water uptake in ancient limestone,

if I sheltered within the niche I built in the wall, hewn
of tufa, Neapolitan, classically pocked and ochered
and proofed against the elements with a bitter amalgam

of fermented cactus, if after all this drudgery the niche
was no larger than a womb in which I had folded myself
like a fetus fully configured, genitalia and cognition formed

and on proffer, as ever, borrowed thoughts, as ever,
on my mind, like the sweetly self-effacing letter Henry James
wrote to William—"when I image those resources of yours

in their large romanticism, I look out of my window
at my so rosy and so mulberried and so swarded garden
with a more consoled sense of its small contractedness"—

I would know only the annealed, the unconsoled surface
of my own contraction, how I abut it on all sides
and within, the same ophidian concretion ossifying

my blood on retinal disk as in clear cornea, as if

I were less pliantly alive, less snake than tesseral snake

on buried mosaic, proffering the first apple to someone,

a woman, a man, an ancestor, unseen because unexcavated.

TAMORA

What cannot be sold is the stillness of the mind
that controls the limb moving in sleep as if running
to escape a terror that turns out to be the curtains,
a gaff of leaves. The left arm is motionless,

and that, too, cannot be sold: it may be concealing
in its crook the swaddled scrap of a baby, the one
who was glimpsed in the arms of its mother
as she ran from mortal fire. The cost of death

is the worldly chill that unnerves your touch
as your lips glance the dead cheeks, the dead mouth,
of a loved one. The otherness is expensive;
it tells you how costly this life is, infinitely more

than the price of a ticket for the slow-motion airplane
as it rips apart, the passenger next to you slipping
into the digital backdrop that contains the vortex
you suffer, too, as a way of passing the time.

Who wouldn't buy the death of strangers, the death
of surrogate selves? Not a pathological pleasure,
the lip smack of a sexual cannibal or the cackle
of a mythic snuff director, but the everyday avenger

who, in popular versions of death, eases the pain
by being cheap and unreal. Never mind part of you
thinks he's unreal but dear. Among the groundlings
you'll stand and watch such atrocities as a great mind

can figure forth. You will hack off the limbs and tongue
of someone whose innocence you've mutilated.
You will feast on a pie containing your own sons.
All for a penny, a penny, among the groundlings.

ON THE BODY'S
IMAGINATION

Imagine the pearl-shaped tumor
behind the eye, snipped away around
the optic nerve, turned into an eye itself,
watching you blindly from the tray.

Imagine the scalpel, the machete,
lolling aside the quadrant of hair,
which flaps and folds back into place
along the suture's nip, as pain drips away.

Imagine the coiled and treacherous
fissure into the brain, the gravity
of its crevasses, blued with the bruise
of thoughts incised by explorers' crampons.

Imagine the sluice of humors round
the murderer's bullet, the surgeon's hand,
except the black wine of melancholy,
inert in the mind's cavernous cellar.

Imagine the chest cleaved open
and a tube convolved into a deep
it should not touch, through packed fibers
of tissue that flinch in the light.

Imagine the heart's numinous glow
fibrillating as you cross the sublime
narthex and naos of a temple
whose faith you can never believe.

Imagine the samlet-sheeted depths
of a solar plexus flensed to expose
a treasure of living mother-of-pearl,
soft and all too easily dissevered.

May nothing mutilate you, nothing
unwhole you, nothing inhabit the moral
of your story, in which you will die
not knowing but supplying, like blood.

AFTERIMAGE

But there was nothing left to do, my friend said,
everything had been done, and being done,
burdened him with the regret of being late, so late

that the chairs were inverted on the café tables
and the loudspeakers on the boulevards
played only the sounds of steel blinds
rolling over the façades of his favorite shops,

and the intersection that he stood at, wondering
where to turn, held nothing but an electric bus,
stranded, abandoned, its swaying antennae
dangling under lifeless wires.

"I want to read books," he said, "only from eras
where polymaths could still learn everything.

"I want to inhabit the corners of ancient maps,
where only the krakens and dragons live."

How could I judge him harshly? How could I say
that everything is being forgotten as we speak,
all the skill of cathedrals and hill towns, the craftsmanship
of insects and tundra, even the human eye

instinct with the unreal stars inside its own orb,
blue spicules of phosphenes, coronal holes
of floaters? How could I tell him we forget
the images in our own eyes?

TO A FUTURE READER

Now that I'm dead I can tell you how I should be read.
The seagull on page 44 was a metaphor.
The valise on the next page was a . . . MacGuffin.
In every detail—a flower, a mother—I was at war
with the literal, except in this sentence.
If I failed to be revelatory when I mentioned the love affair
that ended in a vision of God, forgive me.
As a writer, I looked for revelation in words.

I found no gods in the afterlife, only a purple gloaming
in which twelve-point Garamond scrolls upward
to a rectangle of white radiance that turns out to be
what the afflicted see in Saramago's *Blindness*.

If in life I was ravaged by ambition, which I hid
behind a veneer of insufferable modesty,
I balanced it with a cheerfully desolate solitude
armored against the usual squibs of literary glory,
like a gruesome brawl in a Deptford tavern
or an erotic tiff with my version of Lou Andreas-Salomé.

I know that the outlook for the inner life is bleak,

a Malthusian chart labeled "The Growth of the Inhuman."
Perhaps you're living in a country where reading a book
is an act of transgression. Perhaps you've created
a secret, samizdat archive in a yellow-pastel basement
off Nevsky Prospekt, the black felt boots of passersby
crisscrossing in the windows above. Perhaps
you are the last person who cares about my words at all.
I see you turning the pages tremulously, your gloved hand
holding up a tiny, poignant penlight.

There, let me steady it for you. There, there . . .

QUEUE

Behind you a line has formed of the lost,
the lowly, the desperate. They stretch back
along the shore beyond the fading cliffs.

The wind-up emergency radio in your hands
tells you to stay calm, help is on its way,
the tide will not come in for hours,

but already it is wetting your bare feet.
You help the woman next to you, rolling
her wheelchair a few feet closer to the highway.

She looks up with an expression of gratitude
and fear, as a line of speeding fire trucks
swerves narrowly on her left, blowing her chair

sidelong with the force of their passing.
You tell her not to worry, but now the sea
has drawn closer, and everyone is crowded

on the narrow strip of sand by the highway.
Soon it is dark, and you can hear from behind
the cries of people and the roar of trucks,

and you know soon it will be a massacre,
soon you'll be the only able-bodied person
who can rescue the injured and dying.

You wind the radio, but it only repeats the words,
"Do not panic, help will come," and the woman
in the wheelchair, her face hidden in darkness,

whispers, in your late mother's singsong voice,
"You're wrong. You know what you can bear.
Be strong. You'll find the reason you're here."

REVELATION
The Light

And the sun circles in the sky, and the seas heave their currents
into the air, and the light rains down in arcs upon a dying city
where you lie on your side reading a book about a prince

who no longer believed in the world, not in love, not in family,
not in the afterlife, not in the kingdom he would inherit,
its crumbling chamfers and desiccated moats, its abrogated will.

You read to forget the terrible sunlight burning through your roof,
and the cries for "Water, water!" from all sides,
and the grave face of the child at your doorstep, too parched

to do anything but hold out a little porcelain teacup, an extinct
    flower—
a rose—painted on its side. But you too are dying
of thirst, fragmenting among heat-mirage visions of the flood

as it lapped over the seaside towers, then subsided
to reveal the great cracked lithosphere under the sea,
its fossilized scallops and clypeasters, and the Gothic buttresses

of a human rib cage that, in your own aridity, you recognized
as the skeleton of your father. You know what you need to do,
not to change the recalcitrant powers hovering in their bastions,

but to keep yourself whole even as the world lifts and flurrs
among waves of descending light. You will fashion a radiant crown,
make of yourself a Sol Invictus, out of the only abundance

remaining: that it is nothing but light doesn't matter,
that the only power you possess is the power
to be dispossessed doesn't matter, you have power now

over your own death, its palliative swell, its spinning astrolabe,
its topcastle from which you view with princely disdain
the blue darkness beneath the blue darkness of your spectral sails.

DOUBLE SOUL

You would meet your other soul in his throng of disciples.
You would extend your hand and show mercy on his crimes.
The light would fall before him like the plane of a mirror.
When he touched you, you would feel the sangfroid of glass.

He would dissemble with Delphic concision and chasteness.
His hands would bear etchings of the men he had dispatched.
He would steal your face and expunge it of human luster.
He'd search your eyes for the eudæmon life you failed to live.

If you took his place, the others would see your pretense
of the arcane transgressions he justified to their Baal.
If you took his place, their faith would break like a host
in the mouth of a nonbeliever, desiccate of folly and paste.

By his side is the gray-eyed dog his sole companion,
the only witness to the blood rites that procured his renown.
By his side is the white-fanged wolf his herder of victims,
whose hilltop raptures would sustain the illusion of life.

So you leave him among the dead on the Hill of Vultures,
a point of darkness in an aurora shaped like a crowd.
So you turn your back on the sermon that he murmurs,
your own solitude relayed viva voce among the dead.

By morning you'll return to yourself without premonition
of the death your unreal double would grant by rote.
By morning you'll cease to conflate the taint of dreaming
with the clouds that reflect the sightless glare of rooms.

Now he renews his sunlit presence in the bed beside you,
the dailiness outside the dissonances of your dread.
Now he restores his existence as your only true other,
the beloved who is waiting, waiting to sing in your ear.

THE CHANGES

"... and there, his blood gone mad,
seized a sharp stone,
divorced his vital members from his body."
CATULLUS

In summer, among tide run and neap flat,
he knew the hue of sea under cumulus
and cirrus, the vein of coral strewing foam,
strand's indeterminacies of pulsed grain
where eight certain digits skimmed and skirred
to winged flight, that brushstroke V
convexed in his binoculars' second eyes.
Later, at sundown, he searched field guide
and reference tome to procure the names
of things he learned by sight by day, whether
chromatocentric (slate-blue to cobalt-blue
remiges) or cool and Latinate (*Ardea
herodias*) or plain as vision (blue heron),
each phrase lighting synchronies of mind,
for now or all his life. From this, before
the grained amity of his desk, he knew
the gift of solitude as feathered, spectral
knowledge diminishing wing after wing
through mist and eyeblink, unless fixed
by artifice of lens, then transfixed as words
on paper, sequent, present, in lamplit toil
among the tranquil stanzas of his home.

But in autumn, across the continent,
at a neo-Gothic pile vaster than Bruchion,
where a thousand leaded-glass panes revealed
a sixteen-level stack tower vertiginous
with the world's text, he was lost to words,
lost in the hermeneutics of words, the bird
of meaning receding with Zeno's arrow,
as in the books he once loved without qualm,
which he dissected now as force and ruse,
the blackish squares of Queequeg's tattoos
immuring meaning in a lacuna of male eros,
just as each stunning epigrammatic period
bore the shrieks of rats pithed with *épingles*
as Marcel's depraved proof of depravity,
senseless with senselessness, as meaning
was meaningful with meaninglessness.
With all that he learned to unlearn, he chose
as commencement a desert deprived of texts,
at first deprived of words themselves, among
indigenes sequestered within ritual
and morpheme he memorized each day
until one day the village relinquished
its aspect and names, eloquently imbued

with sacraments of sun and bird and cloud
that beguiled the land with eternal return
to the grass and leaves of bare subsistence,
the selfsame child listless in the dust
as identical flies nictated round its eyes.
Now he taught the succoring technology,
studied with a dozen altruistic youths
in the spring before he flew across the sea,
of "dead level contours" and "infiltration pits,"
of drip formations to green the endless
encroach of whirring sand and aloe waste.
After two years cataphylls unfurled on the stem,
drupelets plumped with daily moisture,
the calyx held its sweet pearl against the sun;
after three, the circle of fire and drought
receded into the sands behind the village,
and he glimpsed, at last, the garden at the end
of enterprise, whose green unguent drift
bespoke the quenched thirst, the unfamished girth,
the beholden heart. When the men opened
a thatched gate to show the occult sanctum
where his last banquet was laid, he bowed
his head ceremoniously, and entered

a torchlit space girded by long wooden tables
heaped with platters of steaming harvest grain
and formal goblets made of gourds brimming
with sweet wine thick as the blood of oxen
and, in a bath of real blood, viscera arrayed
as for a high priestess's haruspication.
There the shamans surrounded him and lifted
to his lips an eggshell of fire-water laced
with bitter morsels striated with the fur
of mold, which he drank reluctantly, queasily,
a dozen brazen hands stroking downward
at his Adam's apple and throat to ensure
he took the full measure: *Oo-koo-he! Oo-koo-he!*
the men warbled like birdsong, as epithet
for the sacred philter. And so the goddess
entered him, entered all the men, who tore off
his clothes and lifted him, naked, shrieking,
to the high table, till his voice, his mind, his eyes
succumbed to hers. In shame he stared down
at the strangeness of his sex, and raised
the pastoral scythe and divorced the members
from his body, and the other divines stanched
the blood with a bolus of cobweb and vetch,

and daubed a live fowl thrashing its wings
across his torso and limbs, which writhed now
with the clear, limitless agony of the gods.
When he awoke, he was alone on a desert shore,
bloodwash and down weaving a sheer chiton
over the scarred otherness between his legs,
and peered across the water to the modern skyline
in a vortex of snow: the bridge's harp and altar,
art deco spires, a single skyscraper contoured
like the frozen flame of a torch, all swirling
in white flurries that the sun burned through,
subsuming him in radiance as it subsumed all
in the indifference of Image—flux of texts
on screens, streaks of sleeve and hair,
scumble of taxis to and from the Temple
of Aspiration—and even Mount Ida,
green phantom flickering behind mammæ
of snowdrift and sleek towers, offered no echo
of bird-trill or dithyramb, indifferent, too,
to the pity he felt for his past selves,
now that he was merely another god,
transformed from nothing into everything,
holding all in one final terrible snowflake.

THE VISITATION OF GOD

My life is over, and I can begin my work.
I will burn all my letters and journals—better yet,
shred them to make confetti for a party
I will never give. No self-pity: I will be too busy.
I will read everything I was too depressed from failed love
to comprehend. I will know the world
through other minds, the best minds, the most gracious,
from times so distant I must summon compassion
to understand the human frailty
beneath the slanted saliences of custom and mores,
and I will find deliverance from the prison
of my assumptions, as one who looks up
from the rocks that he has sundered futilely, to expiate
an inexpiable crime, sees in a sudden downpour
of sunlight the holy balm
that would salve his ragged hands.

I will praise the epiphanies
that arrive with cunning facility in great art
and with awkward and belated affect in everyday life—
the outré grandeur of well-articulated love
or the coincidence in the street that would tie up
all the beggared strands of narrative in one's life—

but I will take pity on the unstoried moments
through which I pass in daily indifference
to their sublimity: the dog rising to the side
of my sickbed to lick my hand once,
with human subtlety, or my father saying in passing,
"I'm on your side." And in deference
to the beauty of silence, I will allow the vision
to rest there, without the constant hectoring
after meaning, the interminable crossing out
and fashioning forth upon proof and page
of yet another mercenary exchange: these words
I sell in complaisance to your eyes.

From this land where every life, in the act
of making a living, implicates itself
in the grand demonic commerce of our age,
where the things I would buy afford no purchase
on the matter of spiritual well-being, and the desire
for the transcendent is engyved with the horrors
committed in the name of ancestral faith
or worldly allegiance, where science itself—
not the unsettled questions of the universe,
like dark energy or the nature of consciousness,

but the scientific method, its looping, retrograde
motion towards metamorphosing certainties—
provides cover for the short-term greed
that enacts the global catastrophe,
where there is no ease of escape or manumission,
not the philanthropist's guilt or the hermit's ordure,
not the working artist's fealty to a medial truth
between the evidence of corruption and the evidence
the corrupt will consume, I will speak
only with blears and temblors of equivocation,
out of humility in tutelage to the god,
who instructs the poorest peasant girl
to withhold all context as she reveals the oracle,
for only those who know themselves can unravel
their good fortune from her ambiguity,
and more than the fall of a kingdom
is at stake. If we inhale the sacred vapors
from the fissure under the temple, we would know
how the act of omission would sustain a space
for the ineffable truths, a last acre
of primeval forest and sun-filtered canopy
not yet slashed and burned by the modish,
the literal, the militantly underwhelmed.

You, you, whose very being examples
omission as the highest form of existence,
you whose ceaseless abjurations teach
the fearful child to pray ardently within your silence,
I would surrender myself as I did then,
as if your voice inhabited my meager questions.
In the new world, would thousands cease to die
in your name? Would the oceans hover in the sky
and circle your face? And if you chose
to create a place without suffering, would we,
sic vita est, no longer exist? Forgive me, Lord,
for failing to conjure an image of the strange
and sublime creatures you would devise
in our stead, who visit me only
as exquisite figments of cloud or motes
of wisdom and bliss through which transpierce,
without pain or human love, the tines
of earthly fire, the microcosmic cusps
of rain and dust.

DIVINE FIRE

(AFTER LUIS CERNUDA'S
"*APOLOGIA PRO VITA SUA*")

Open the doors. Let everyone return.
How rare they've always been.
There's room to spare inside my love.
For many years no one has entered,
like a house the owner abandoned,
exiled to other lands. Nothing
overturns the clandestine rule
of mouse and moth and spiderweb,
except the rays of the sun, slyly filtering
through cracks in the attic blinds
to shake the sleep of dust from bleary contours,
or the hawthorn laden with spring flowers,
infected with the wind's madness,
rapping on windowpanes that stare blindly
at dawn's sunlit pearl or the amber moon.

Now bring them closer to my bed.
Turn the light on their faces, like stars
suspended in the night over black water.
The agony of him who loves them unites them,
though they remain unknown to each other,
immured together only in my memory.
First, you, Archangel, take my hand,
because I no longer know if I loved or hated you,

and forgiveness is the only thing that matters
before I surrender my soul. Even now oblivion
steps closer, past the ruin of walls and sentries.
If love isn't a word, a futile encounter of the lips,
the way fingers fix a translucent wing
under the curious lens in some laboratory,
I believe I loved you. But it no longer matters.

Let those return who took your place
in your absence, just as the death of the king
invested the sword and crown in another,
trumpets resounding to the moon in jubilee,
although the new monarch soon discovered
the primal legacy of that hero too much to bear.
In elevating himself, he raised his successors
in name, but not in the passion of rulers.
But isn't passion the measure of the grandeur
of man, and the soul's glory a tempering
of steel in fire? The other bodies taught me
that if love languishes and I no longer believe
in the truth of him I love, desire grows stronger,
vanquishing with fire all forebodings
of the hopeless many I'd consign to hell.

It's your turn to come, friends.
How clearly I recall what these eyes tell:
if the desert sun ravages you, enter here.
I'll bestow the gift of repose on you.
Marriages of shadow and light create a penumbra
favorable for idle confidences, and everything
awaits the new visitor: a glass of wine,
a comfortable chair, white lilacs drowsing
in a corner. A tender spell of bonhomie
would salve a body that had sojourned alone
in the nightless desert. After purgatory,
even limbo is a pleasure. So trust the gesture
of fraternity, yours if you forsake passion,
even if one day I vanquish your memory
with my own forgetfulness.

Yes, you were right, my friends.
There's no higher truth than oblivion.
Of all the years that have passed, holding
the sum of my life, the only memories
that remain are those destined to die
as I forget, just as a candle that burns
in a cave casts its final shadows on the wall.

I safeguard them, as some safeguard
their love, ambition, even their contempt.
But these memories are trifles. And from them—
untold dreams emerging from the gates of horn
or the fervid nightmare from the gates of ivory—
the last shades mournfully ascend,
shades of the men in my blood,
pleading for a sanction the soul disavows.

The journey to death is no easy matter,
and if living is hard, dying is no less so.
Others might relieve the pain of arrival
at that finish line, stretching the ribbon,
breaking the tape, of consciousness itself.
Incorruptible, they did not witness what I saw,
the acrid victory of death as they relinquished
their souls with unthinking goodbyes.
I contemplate my own death, a broken wing
that has fallen to earth but struggles still,
feathers no longer sustained on the air.
How beautiful the light appears now,
shaking in the blue aureole behind branches,
dun-brown in winter, where the ice glows.
Renouncing the light is harder than death itself.

I have only this to say: I am burdened by sins
I had neither occasion nor power to commit.
I lived without you, my Lord, who would not aid me
when disbelief tormented my soul.
I come before you now, vanquished, easy prey
for your ministers, whose lifted hands
pardon or condemn the acts of man.
But who is a man to judge men?
Faithless prayer doesn't cure the afflicted,
but those who sin will be forgiven.
A kiss on the lips of that dark olive oil,
whose virtue anoints the warrior
and the dying man, can still seal the grace
of this body, its elements already
reverting to earth, water, air, and fire.

It is right that the blood of the earth
daubs and pardons the one approaching death,
however blurry and half-opened the portals
that lead to his senses. With purest oil
a finger traces the enchanted sign on eyes
that gazed at beauty and light, coveting them;
on the ear, a conch enfolding voice and song;
on the curve of nostrils open to the perfume

of spikenard, the aroma of the body and of rain;
on the mouth, which sang and kissed and lied;
on hands that sifted through silk and coin;
on the back in spasm, a quavering bole.
Just as a bird's flight sketches in the air
not the form of the wing but its ephemeral wake,
memories vanish in the cloud of my mind.

To die, man does not need God,
but God needs man in order to exist.
When I die, will the dust give praise to God?
Will it be the dust that declares his truth?
Once the image is lost, the mirror goes blind.
Don't destroy my soul, O Lord,
if the hand that crafted a soul can unmake it.
Rescue it with your love. Don't let the cunning
of darkness prevail over it. Temper my soul
with divine fire until one day it is rendered
unto the light you make. My Lord, if you willed
that no one shall be desolate who trusts in you,
then after this starless night the dawn will come,
and we will find in you our resurrection and life.
Now let the light enter in. Open the doors.

ON THE DESIRE TO
BE FREE OF A PERSONA

Like the chaos of maelstrom or the dolor of doldrum,
the orange sulfur that vents from Io's infernal calderas
or the haze from Kalimantan or Mumbai that exhales

across the ocean to suffuse the seagull-tinted clarities
off Cape Mendocino; like air so pristine it's more
the vacua of space, the tenuous solitude of plasma

or the eerie wind beyond the heliopause, even the enigma
of dark energy, so abstruse that constants or quintessences
are conjured to make it real; like air and space, then,

but also fire, earth, and water, especially the way
all forms of water motion against the contours of things,
clear water that sleeks over purple-eyed nudibranch

on a dying reef in Australia, or blue ice that sheers off a crevasse
above Qaanaaq where the narwhal swim, or steaming water
braiding sun-strands of sunflare-red and coronal blue

at a prismatic spring in Yellowstone: to refract not one
but all aspects of the world, all larks and variations,
all metaphors and exaltations, in this, my only life.

THE AROMA FROM
AN UNSEEN BAKERY

There are days when the senses resist the influx of air
and light, when the girt middle of a cloud collides
with the child who thought he was flying a kite,
when the sculptor Time takes a nap
in the unfinished colonnade, and all is freeze-frame
and dissolve, belying the parallel tradition
that the world is time-lapse: your yawning childhood,
the books you skimmed, the long hours of avoirdupois
and desiderata, the comfort meal repeated
and repeated on a dining table that shape-shifts
from something broad and familial into something
lean and solitary. When did you learn the desperation
of tables and the cries of comedians in their sleep?
When did you discover the unseen, the transparent,
among the solid geometries of car doors, food stamps,
brute affluence, feckless pilasters? By accident,
you veer off into a side street so lovely—
the golden light of a summer evening, lindens,
porches full of slow-dancing youths—
you no longer worry if the warmth you feel
as you turn the corner comes from the great ovens
that hold the next morsel you will savor
or the entrance to the seventh circle of hell.

Even now the view is coming into focus,
the luminous rectangle of the frosted window
homely and inviting. The fragrance of almonds,
of butter, of yeast, enters you. You step forward,
your hand forever pressing the latch of the door.

ON VIEWING
MY FUNCTIONAL MRI

I crossed the willed topography of the light
into a blue vascular space whose shadows told
a tale of latency and subsense,

until a thought flooded with amber light
a swarm of pixels, saying, Here's the childish picture
of a boat on a sea, here a young prince,

here the soprano voice of the clinician
commanding me not to move, not to nod asleep.
Here is sleep, far from placid or quiescent,

blue jets, red pulse elves, sprite halos,
as glimpsed from a geo-stationary satellite
above the tempest that Ariel made.

WINDLESTRAE

A calf's skull, remnants of brindled hide,
the field's lavish aridity spotted with purples,
bull's-eyed, parched, under noonday arrows;
spoor of cougar, spoor of man;
a hiking boot's mudded archipelago,
dried and flaking in a sea of dry air,
now evidence of something ancient,
one who walked here a day ago, a world ago—

when you have finished your wanderings,
will you find the place that always existed after,
after drought, after the end, where to move
is to blur like a life snapped at the wrong aperture
and to stay in place is to narrow the prism
to a sublime wavelength, your bloom
so memorably hued a stranger will lean
into the lost corolla as if to remember
what she can no longer scent.

PESSOA

Inside the selves we knew were another and another.
One drained us of blood, one infused us drop by drop.
Years faltered on a fractal's iterations.
At the end, a mirror held an image of the sea.

We reached in. Our hands vanished into the frame.
Concentric circles whispered, "Echo, echo, echo. . . ."
When we withdrew our fingers, they dripped on stone
a scent of brine, the touch of a wave.

I was the son my mother never had.
You were an aspect of myself that I never acted on.
From the threshold I waved to you goodbye.
In your car you drove to the fatal crash.

I praised you with the eulogy you had written for me.
You leaned over the coffin and kissed my cheek.
Among the flowers was an arrangement of stars,
which was the night we drank *vinho verde* on the piers.

Against the Tagus the green-yellow bottle was lambent,
with a ghostly afterglow, like the light at dusk.
A blue shadow of marijuana trailed a drowsy teenager.
You spoke of déjà vu, which made me laugh.

From a high window under a jacaranda cloud
a mournful fado ended with a crescendo of cheers.
The merchant vessel docking in the black harbor
became a convent ruined in Voltaire's earthquake.

At a shop window on the Rua da Misericórdia,
we stared and stared at an illuminated globe,
as if a world reduced to bright quintessence
had gathered the sublime from our humble fragments.

But there were only the two of us walking in the city,
and the shade of a poet, who, no longer living,
had no need for his aloneness, but joined us anyway,
to satisfy himself that the dead could still feel alone.

IN PRAISE OF DISQUIET

The years are fine with dust that settles in the eyes.
The stars are bound to gods from abandoned temples.
By night you fear the abdication of the sun.
By day you wear the light like a broken crown.

Silence, stillness, absence pass, pass and murmur
themselves into sound, and music is simple
on a tinkling harpsichord that troubles the ear
with the drone of a word no tongue can tell.

How can you measure the self's impulse to savage
the truth in the name of ordinary, sensuous joy?
Would you rather live outside your own body,
high above the griffon's wing, in an ultraviolet field?

There is nothing that exists that isn't intractable,
not this glass of water, not the tears of a child.
The loose-leaf notebook flung for effect over a cliff
will tell the truth to the ink-stained sea, line by line.

Let death be an aspect of travel, a vessel tossed
on a horizon from which another universe obtrudes,
a wood-grained tedium that blesses the event horizon
with the somnolence of mercy for a self departed.

Be delirious in negation, conjuring blank images
to find within the stillness of your meditative brow
an answer silhouetted against the mind's terraces—
and say *No* to it, since it is yours, limned with doubt.

The mouse twitters freely across the rooftop.
The owl is unreal that perches on the parapet.
The lovers lying in a blanket on the fire escape
let fall through the grates a page of their aubade.

You live in mission, in solitary devoir, for the time
you no longer need a maple leaf, a morning face,
to fracture the sense of unbelief into song.
Imagine the songless stranger who lives next door.

EGG

If you touch me, I crumble. I'm a man of dust.

Touch is one medium, thought another.

If I think of you, I turn to dust.

When did my life never empty into heaven?
Grace that my substance remains mortal and local.

Each clayey digit points towards earth,
which holds no hell left uncharted
by *The Garden of Earthly Delights*.

The thought of you is a green thing in the earth.

It spins round and round and lies naked
in a shallow stream singing of radical freedom:

the art of being stripped of all traces of the earth.

So I lie next to you there, parts of me washing away
and commingling with you.

Nothing comes of this mud but what is deposited
there, in our absence, in our mortality,

by all mortal beings that fly and crawl and stray.

Their eggs, too, are made of dust.

Open one, and it spills an earthbound light.

THE DEATH OF
THE TELEGRAM

They had resisted the point as they flecked
what wasn't yet a spear. Then the point existed.
The beveled shards fell away. The prey dropped heavily
on its side. The hafted idea formed at Levallois—
the sequence that only a tipping scale of brain mass
could enumerate—traveled hand to hand, land to land,
as a stain on an engored mouth.

Sometimes I dream a man exists behind the doorbell.
He wears a uniform. He holds a yellow envelope.
I sign something. I hold out a dollar, which he takes.
Through the envelope I can see the words.
Someone has died, someone I care for, someone who existed
before I was born, who went away to a war,
someone that I sent a blanket to, a book of poems.
It was an era where soldiers read poems
without shame. STOP.

On the other side of the world an earthquake levels
a city built of flimsy concrete stacks set into muddy hills,
and a child is born in a tent, and a grandfather
borrows pennies from the other refugees
so that he can trudge through the ruins
with an old literate woman, who will write

the simple paragraph that will tell his ancient village
that joy follows sorrow, sorrow follows joy,
nothing exists without mercy,
no mercy exists without sorrow.

I am waiting among the flickering stars on the porch step
as the flurry of activity within attests to the absence
of a household god or a wayward premonition
that chitters through the frightened inhabitants.
But when the door opens, there is only a child, a little girl,
and I ask, "Where are your parents?" The little girl
does not answer, so I repeat, "Where are your parents?"
The little girl looks down, expressionless, heavy-lidded,
inscrutable, like a lost head from Phidias's Fates.
Soon I realize that the envelope in my hands
contains the answer.

GENERATIONS

Someday, when you have grown tall, you will find
that I have grown small, and so many of your friends
will abide by rules that I have long forgotten
that you will think I am doddering and unmoored,

like a flibbertigibbet of crumpled paper
as the wind toys with it, pushing it
in decrepit zigzags along the boardwalk.

And it is true that I no longer find solace
in the lights and din of the carnival. I am standing
so far away that it is a mere gaudery
of colored lights from which emerges a child,

crying and bleating for its mother. I am trying to cross
the sand to help the child, but as I reach the apex
of the next dune, I find myself on another shore.

I can see only sand and ocean and a distant kayak
in which you labor against a swell that pushes you back
with each paddle forward. I call out to you,

but you can't hear me, and in any case, what can I do
to help? You wouldn't listen to my advice anyway:

Stop paddling. Go back. What you were told
was wrong. Everything doesn't lie ahead. Everything
is behind, behind. I exist to tell you so.

GENERATIONS

The It-Factor swagger, the mimic rebellion, the loutish
tropes in a glut of beauty, slavishly repeat your past.
Their conformities came clear only when you lost It.
Now envy desires the body, not the ejecta of the mind.

Would they hear if you told them? As the modish packs
loiter by, you dematerialize within their unitasking gaze.
Limpid jets of selfhood stain dating app or foodie truck.
They sing their dullness electric. "Our dullness is better,"

they sing. Weren't *you* better? The body's pride craved more,
which defiled you, too, and you thirsted after many vessels—
mouths, ventricles—and tippled therefrom, and they you,
until you thought, dully, "It'll soon be over." And it was.

Now they command the culture, the commodified torsos,
faces that declaim, with unlined lubricity, nothing matters
but a certain snark and slickness to stamp out slo-mo Art.
Complain, and you're dubbed out of your own podcast.

You'd rise up, but you're weary, and they know it. Already
they patronize the old folk's home you erect in your mind.
When they fluff your pillows, you graze some proximate skin,
but it cringes with gooseflesh as at a giallo-flick corpse.

DESPOND

A Slough

I am a prodigy of despair.
In the womb I wailed the maternal night away,
gurgling like a monkfish under water.
My Francophile parents nicknamed me "Triste,"
although my schoolmates called me "Killjoy."
At age ten I wrote a book of epigrams
titled "Despond: A Slough."
Sample: "Time teaches us that happiness is nothing
more than an early phase of sorrow."
During puberty my clothes were covered
in grass stains from the hours I spent
writhing in torment *en plein air*.
From that angle my father's lawn mower
made a grimace of "existential nausea,"
a cliché I knew could never replicate
the immanent sadness of inanimate objects.
In college I played the saxophone
because it had so many sad tone holes
over which my numb fingers glumly riffed
Coltrane's "I Want to Talk about You."
I always stopped in the middle of the cadenza
because I never wanted to talk about you.
Was there a "you" anyway?

Or were you always dead air?
I see your deep ungulate eyes filling with tears
as you ask me over and over, in a hundred
bars and cafés and museum galleries,
"Are you happy? Are you happy?"
Enough already! I'm happy as a blue juniper berry
plucked from an ancient juniper bush
that gets passed from hand to filthy hand
only to end up in a sentimental drunk's
sloshing martini glass.
Didn't you ever think the point of life
was to become the purest distillate of dolor,
to flee the psychiatrist's office in tears
and fling the free sample pack
of μ-opioid receptor agonists
down the nearest storm drain?
I thought not. Adieu, adieu, happy one,
already moving on to happier lovers
and lower-maintenance minds in uncluttered
apartments where the only thing blue
is the blue Bauhaus sofa
with the basset hound dozing on top.

AUTOBIOGRAPHY OF
MY SERIOUSNESS

Once I was a mere tonality,
then I became an alternative lifestyle.
All forms of hipness entered my grinder
and squeezed out a transparent sausage,
which I popped to release the hot air.
Some years I hid inside your rucksack
with the antiquated pens and pads,
untouched but for the lists
of failed New Year's resolutions.
While you were having fun, I calculated
an eleemosynary tithe for the hours you wasted
frolicking with your lovers and friends.
You scoffed at my list of charities, saying,
"I can barely cover the rent, *dissipateur*!"
but you bowed to my suggestion
of sunset and a snick of Parmenides.
A rose-colored cloud asked gravely,
"What is the nature of Being?"
but you couldn't wrap your ADHD
around the question, despite my
and Matthew Arnold's help.
To evade the tedium of thinking,
you threw a home-entertainment tantrum,

fixating on the hit streaming series *Seriously, Will!*,
which followed a troupe of actors
as they scrounged up money
for some free plays in the park.
You loved the antics of Will and Rosa
and Cleo and Chris and company,
but after all the struggles to paint the flats,
the *pièce de résistance* was always the climactic
soliloquy, that slow zoom out
from the actor's face, declaiming lines
of immortal eloquence just for you,
as the audience rose to its feet
in an elm-fringed meadow. Even I,
chariest of all, whistled and hooted.

THE DECLINE AND FALL
OF MY SELF-CONSCIOUSNESS

No, I didn't know myself.
I was a little honey mushroom
sprouting above the giant fungus
in the Malheur National Forest.
Under my body something implacable
and monstrous shifted with each
glum notion, each tut-tut movement.
As I strolled, I felt my feet cling
to my ankles, my steps lurch upward
in serial dorsiflexion. The characters
on my cuneiform bones implored,
"Improve, improve," and soon
I was making an unscheduled pratfall
down the stairs of the Science Center,
a folly shaped like a Polaroid Land camera.
I couldn't take a picture without a shudder
or shutter of self-imputation.
Snapshot: "View of Childhood as Hand
Sweeping Back Lock of Hair in Eyes."
Snapshot: "View of Adolescence
as Hand Pushing Glasses Up Nose."
Books offered the transitory glamour
of an otherness without the thought
of the thought of self-reflexiveness.

In the parable by Kafka Trismegistus
the man who stood before the mirror
that contained all the world's wisdom
desired only to ensure that the silvering
would last. Knowledge would die
when the reflection veined and webbed
and splotched the text with the features
of some dead chimera, like a papyral
palimpsest through which the mummy
slowly materialized. In real life,
the mirror was nailed to the ceiling
of our room in some red-velvet motel.
All those limbs moving in unison
to a throbbingly vulgar bass beat!
And the only thing we learned from love
was the art of becoming another.
Turn off the subwoofer, Love,
what remains is something wee,
wee and oh-so-sempiternal, the self
unselfing another, world without end.

FRAGMENTS FROM
MY LOST YEARS

There was an ellipsis in the sentence.
The space between two clouds intervened.
I wept privately over small things: chipping
an old tea cup, finding a dead sparrow.
If I wrote the history of those years—
not that I ever would.
My kindness took the form of avoiding people;
I did not want to alter their lives for the worse.
This is the way emptiness reasons.
I walked and walked, to the sea, through the city,
in the woods. I thought the landscape
would tell me how to continue.
It told me to continue to walk.
In my spare time I plotted against my unreal enemies.
The perfect revenge involved a disguise,
a stakeout, a closet, and some pills in açai juice.
But vengeance had become too popular,
and I was a nonconformist.
True, the god Disquiet was infinitely portable.
At times he lived on the dusty top of a bookshelf.
At other times he impaled himself on my keychain.
One day I saw him in the flag on a flagpole
and in the elderly man below saluting the flag.

In a puddle I saw his youthful face,
ravaged by fire and lust,
like Iasion after the thunderbolt.
When I swallowed him in the form of a pill,
he disappeared forever into my liver, my gall,
all my anachronistic humors.
I asked a new friend where I was,
and she told me, kindly, that I was elsewhere.
The young man under the stairs
invited me in to wear his shoes.
I did, oh I did.
In my hands I held a sphere of light that said,
"You are merely a god who will die."
When I released it, it rose high into the air,
burst and rained on a rock in the water
where some sea lions rested.
They started at the falling stars—
a hundred eyes turned in unison—
then they swam away.

ON THE SUPERIOR
INTELLIGENCE OF OTHERS

They look at you, the gods, knowing what you think before
    you do,
and like a god, you mustn't show your ignorance: be perceptive,
because what matters is that you know the names of songs, of
    stars.

They see into the ancient tablet the melody it hums, they see
    into the lens
the red-shifted implication. They would interpret your blank
    stare
as they look at you, knowing what you don't know before you
    can learn it.

They know the patterns of social recognition, the embattled
    aspiration
of your natural narcissism towards furtiveness or denial:
"As if what matters is that I know the names of songs or stars!"

True, the facts matter less than the larger picture, even if the
    larger picture
is a refuge to which you withdraw, as into a dark cave without
    shadows,
far from the eyes of those who look at you, knowing you before
    you do.

The gods would strike you down for your ignorance, however
    culpable,
however aleatory, because everything you don't know is
    evidence
of disbelief, the narrowness that ignores the origins of songs
    and stars.

I'm not smarter than you. How can you judge such things?
    You know things
I don't know, and vice versa. They're as insecure as you, the
    solipsists
who stare like false idols, miming prescience of what you
    think and do,
lisping arcana—Ugarit tablet, GN-ZI 1—to belittle your songs
    and stars.

MY FUTURE,
WITH A FADED VERMEER

I am alone, then more alone.
Laughing, I accept my lot as choice or fate,
flicking through the obituaries like a card sharp.
My wrinkles form a pattern of resolute sadness,
my sublunary scalp gray with moondust.
The ghost of my mother slaps me across the face
to rouse me from my stupor, but I feel nothing:
she no longer haunts me.
I nod and rake the garden of autumn leaves.
Soon I will curl in them like a malamute in snow.
In my dreams purple-blue irises close
like the eyes of lovers reclining on white gurneys
in an endless procession.
Guy is clutching a wilted bouquet as he says,
"Please stop remembering me. Goodbye."
Now I rise and rise again from a wide bed
chosen for its square divergence
from the shape of a coffin.
Each day I stand before a wall with three views
like a homely triptych: a window with a dawn sky
and an illumined bat that flickers
through an intricate polystyrene cloud,
vaulted, with weak zygomatic arches,

like the braincase of an extinct rodent;
then the artist, turned away, sketching
the model in the voluminous blue dress—
her allegorical bugle, his luminous brushstroke—
but yellowed, lachrymal, as if the hope
I once purchased at the Met poster shop
had come to immortal grief.
In the last panel a still-youthful man laughs
at the elderly face in his mirror and says,
with pained and anachronistic conviction,
"Be grateful, Lord, you have time to waste."

THE DEATH OF
THE MAN WHO WAS A GOD

Then the sea of shadows will flicker over him like the face
of a tree, softly, without pain, releasing each expression of leaf
with a touch. Memory will be a comet that, as it moves closer,
becomes the tailed augur of his recognitions. In ignorance,
he will throw stones that return to the earth
as falling stars. One will blind him with a flash of light,
and he will recognize all that his transformation had lost.

You move through the darkness remembering your immortality,
how the saturated hues of the changing sky held a vision
of the interior of your eye, its rods and cones
momentarily reflecting the sunlit stream, the clouds
like ripened fruit, the blood on your hands that vanished
under a spiral of water. Nothing could wound, not the stones
within the shallow stream, not the smiles of the other gods.
Only now are you enfeebled, breathing the labored air
while remembering the soulful clarity of a young god's lungs.

In this way he is transformed again. The unpruned poplars
of memory return, and the rust-colored road, and the ancient faces
of those who have forgotten life. The swell of the sea inhabits him.
He is alive now to tell the others about the return voyage
of gods, of immortality. He opens his mouth to speak.

Everyone will hear of the triumph that awaits them,
like a broken ship that the waves slowly assemble again
in the blood-dark sea, hammering rusted nails into broken planks,
until the sails billow to the west, to the uninhabited world.

But the languor of his tongue is a sparrow's wing that a child
ties to a stake in the earth. He is always on the verge
of flying on the sea of air. But no one would listen if he spoke,
or if he spoke, they would mistake it for the song of birds,
of the wind. And when he breaks free from his meager restraints,

he will circle above the faces of his loved ones, like something tiny,
with a tiny agitated heart, that provokes joy if it is noticed,
then sadness, then indifference.

DIVINE FIRE

"No more apocalypses!" the fanatics never cry.
Extinction is bliss for those who resent human life.
How else to be happy when a caul of anger
occludes the prospect of your faith? Better

to enfranchise corruption. Defile the good land.
Pray the Rapture saves your grandchildren
before the tipping globe melts. That ancient image
you worshiped, now haloed, now scimitared,

will strain through Time's wasp-waisted birth canal,
extruding some modish thing, spiteful, vain,
frontotemporally deranged. Tell yourself
He is the Man. Rejoice as He pries the world apart.

This is the end, you'll surmise, the end of dalliance,
of amity, the last gasp of afflatus, of consequent sorrow.
Watch as He scythes the last wheat, which flies
like the severed heads of infidels. Then why does the bread

we break savor of no body but the embodied ghosts
of ancient grass? What infinity lives in the turning leaves
but a vaulted vision of our bonhomie? What life
basks at this homely fire but sees Saoshyant's flame?

The embers will hold an American absence, ashes that leave no mark of ankh or ensō on him who frees critical mass from a nuclear drone. The last cloud will rain fire on flesh that chars to faithless marrow. Even now the soul is fugitive.

Acknowledgments

I am grateful to the following publications where poems first appeared, sometimes in different form:

> The *Asian American Literary Review, Epoch,* the *Georgia Review, Literary Imagination, Margie, Michigan Quarterly Review,* the *New England Review,* the *New Republic, Parnassus, Poetry Northwest, Raritan,* the *Threepenny Review,* and *TriQuarterly.*

The quotation in "The Death of the Family Poem" is from a letter by Henry James to his brother William dated July 18, 1909, near the end of their lives together. William James died on August 26, 1910, and Henry James died in 1916. Quoted from *William and Henry James: Selected Letters,* edited by Ignas K. Skrupskelis and Elizabeth M. Berkeley (Charlottesville: University Press of Virginia, 1997).

The quotation of Catullus in "The Changes" is from poem 63, *The Poems of Catullus,* translated by Horace Gregory (New York: Covici-Friede, 1931).

"The Death of the Man Who Was a God" was inspired by Cesare Pavese's "Mito" from *Lavorare stanca* (1943), translated as "Myth" by William Arrowsmith in *Hard Labor* (Baltimore: Johns Hopkins University Press, 1979).

I would like to express my gratitude to those whose presence and generosity at crucial junctures in my life made my work as a poet possible: Gerald Maa, Jonathan Spence, Stephen Sandy, John Ashbery, Arturo Islas, Diane Middlebrook, Kathleen McClung, Maggie Weshner, Cory Wade, Leonard Nathan, Denise Levertov, James Richardson, Kang-I Sun Chang, Edna Webb, Ann Tully, Michael S. Harper, and Alice Quinn.

GEORGIA REVIEW BOOKS

What Persists:
Selected Essays on Poetry from
The Georgia Review, 1988–2014
BY JUDITH KITCHEN

Conscientious Thinking:
Making Sense in an Age of Idiot Savants
BY DAVID BOSWORTH

Stargazing in the Atomic Age
BY ANN GOLDMAN

Hong Kong without Us: A People's Poetry
EDITED BY THE BAUHINIA PROJECT

Hysterical Water: Poems
BY HANNAH BAKER SALTMARSH

Divine Fire: Poems
BY DAVID WOO